In His Grip

Stories From The Heart of the Streets

MICHAEL McMILLAN

md
PUBLISHING

First published 2015 by Malcolm Down Publishing Ltd.
www.malcolmdown.co.uk

British Library Cataloguing in Publication Data

A catalogue record for this book is available from the British Library

ISBN 978-1-910786-03-1

Photographs used by permission from Think Stock, Getty Images, iStock and
by David Forsyth, David Barron, Andrew Barron.
Front cover photograph by Michael McMillan
Lyrics reproduced by permission of Michael McMillan

Printed in the United Kingdom

Contents

Pastor James Glass

"It goes without saying that music is one of the most influential mediums in contemporary culture. In his music Michael has drawn deeply on his own personal experience to produce lyrics that resonate with sympathy for those who are struggling, and which reveal his own deep faith in God and the reservoirs of God's grace that he has discovered on his journey. You'll find the classic themes of loss and redemption, despair and hope, sin and forgiveness, shame and grace. It's all here!"

[James Glass is Senior Pastor of Glasgow Elim Church]

www.glasgowelim.org.uk

John Robinson

"Michael's life is a testament to God's grace, mercy and love. Michael's heart to change lives through his music, songs and lyrics is extraordinary. Ten years ago we talked on the phone and yet, ten years on, God has taken us both on an incredible journey. You might never know the seeds that you plant when you share your story about God's amazing grace. Michael is living proof of God's great love and it's a privilege to know him. Thinking about his life Isaiah 61 comes to mind. I thank God for you, Michael, and your family. God bless you."

[John Tobinson is the author of *Nobody's Child*, *Somebody's Child* and co-Founder/Director of Place of Grace Ministry Thailand Mission]

www.placeofgracebangkok.org

www.tearstoyoureyes.com

jrsomebodyschild@hotmail.com

Graeme Duffin

"I have known Michael McMillan for many years and it was obvious from the beginning that he has a passion and a heart for those who face major social and personal difficulties and struggles. These are situations that (if we're honest), any of us could find ourselves in, given a different set of circumstances. Michael clearly has a deep faith in God and the commitment he displays to ensuring that this faith is integral to lifestyle choices and the ongoing work that he does, speaks volumes. The songs themselves are all borne out of relationship, experience and love for his fellow travellers in this world, and ultimately love for God. Michael's songs cover a wide range of issues and experiences which cannot fail to move

people who share a common love, and will surely encourage those who are themselves struggling. I pray this book will be a blessing to many."
[Graeme Duffin is a member of Wet Wet Wet, a renowned and highly respected producer, engineer, musician and co-owner of Foundry Music Lab]
www.foundrymusiclab.com
info@foundrymusiclab.com

Fraser Speirs
"I have known Michael both as a friend and as a fellow musician. I had the pleasure of producing his first solo album, *Cold and Roofless*, about ten years ago and it was so evident that Michael had an amazing gift for lyrics and telling 'real' stories through these lyrics. I have watched Michael develop this gift over the years as a songwriter and I know that his songs, music and stories have touched many lives. Michael's faith is clearly apparent in the way he lives his life and in the way he treats his fellow man. He has a real passion for the topics and people he writes about and I am delighted to have travelled part of this journey with him."
[Fraser Speirs is a professional musician/session musician, record producer, virtuoso harmonica player and music teacher]

Mike Krause
"I am proud and honoured to write this commendation for my friend Michael McMillan. I first met Michael 38 years ago when he came to me to study the arts of Taekwondo and Jun Fan Gung Fu (Jeet Kune Do). Michael is one of my intellectual warriors and he has developed his musical gifts with the same great creativity with which he studied martial arts. Today, when I listen to his lyrics they hit the strings of my heart and I find his music truly uplifting. Love and respect my old friend."
[Mike Krause is an internationally acclaimed martial arts instructor. He has also worked as a fight scene stunt coordinator within the film industry. His passion, integrity and highly motivational work ethic make him an exceptionally sought after instructor]
www.mikekrausemartialarts.co.uk

I was born on 22nd May 1956 in Glasgow and brought up (or should I say dragged up, kicking and screaming) in a Jewish family. My father (who was a musician, sportsman and gambler) committed suicide and my mother re-married, changing my name from Silverstein to McMillan. My step-father and I never ever got on. He did his best, I think, but it was just not meant to be.

I hated my childhood apart from the times (most weekends) that I spent with my grandfather, "Grandpa Jack". He was a very kind man who taught me all about music. He brought the music to life and I still miss him today. He had worked in the shipyards but, in spite of that tough lifestyle, had a real gentleness and kindness and he was a man of integrity and great wisdom.

I really hated my school life too! The Jewish people and their children did not accept me, since my name was McMillan. They told me I "wasn't Jewish". There was a lot of anti-Semitism around at that time and non-Jewish people/children didn't accept me as I "was" a Jew.

I ran away from home, school and family when I was 15 and never gave it a second thought. But "God had other plans for me" and I returned, for a short while at least. That school had a fire and I wasn't the least bit upset about that.

Fighting was second nature to me and I became good at it. I hated religion and everything it stood for. Living in the West of Scotland, and especially Glasgow, I did not have to look far to find religion and the bigotry, hatred and violence it often produced. I turned away from it as fast as I could and took the only road I knew – fighting – this time through martial arts training and boxing (I still keep my hand in!), and of course, my real love ... music.

My Grandfather had taught me how to appreciate all kinds of music, from classical to popular and everything in between. I joined a pipe band playing pipes and felt part of a "family". But I also learned to play the drums at the same time and this was the instrument that took me to London and helped me to rebuild my life. You see, in music, no one cares or asks what religion you are, what colour you are. They don't care what size you are, what age you are or what social background you come from – if you can play, you're in. Music was and is a great leveller; it makes all people equal. It's not about fame. When a young child picks up a pair of drumsticks or a guitar or whatever, it's to feel part of something, to feel wanted, to feel accepted. It's never about fame.

At 13 I was fortunate enough to play with the pipe band in a show at the Glasgow Alhambra Theatre, which was being hosted by the late great Frankie Vaughan. Frankie, a Leeds boy, had a real soft spot for Glasgow and wanted to do as much as he could to stop the gang violence and help the young people of the city. It was a great show with many well known names from the world of show business. There was a band called *Marmalade* on the show and when I saw them and heard their great songs and music, I knew instantly that this was what I was going to do. So I played drums in some local bands until I was old enough to leave home – legally this time!

I went to London with a good friend of mine and fellow band member, Brian Robertson. Brian joined Thin Lizzy and achieved great fame and notoriety as one of the best guitar players of that time. I played with a number of the bands and artists of that era and got involved in a lot of things that I shouldn't have, often to excess, but time, space and confidentiality does not allow for further comment on that. Suffice to say that a great time was had by all, well most of the time!

I remember praying to "something or someone" during that time to keep me safe ... and they did. I had no idea who or what I was praying to, "but God had other plans for me."

Eventually, I returned to Glasgow and continued playing drums with local bands and musicians, some who experienced a great deal of record company interest. We gigged and toured, but when push came to shove, as is the way, nothing much happened!

I worked within the motor industry on and off for a number of years, with Porsche and Ferrari, and hated it.

I got married and had/have two wonderful children, and joined the Police Force serving in Inverness and Edinburgh. On nightshifts, especially in the Wester Hailes area of Edinburgh, I would pray to "something or someone" again (although by now I was pretty sure it was God, whatever He or that was) to bring me home safely, and again, He always did.

I got back into music as a drummer in, ironically, a really good Thin Lizzy tribute band called Black Rose and we played all over the place. The band still exists to this day.

I then left the Police, went off the rails completely, made a total mess of my life, got divorced, and drifted from place to place and from job to job, before starting a brand new career as an addictions counsellor, which I still do. As a Police Officer I could understand why a single parent living on the 16th Floor of a multi-storey block of flats might shoplift to survive and although it was wrong and a crime had been committed, I took no pleasure in charging people with some offences. It was also very obvious to me that many people in "Great Britain" do not start on a level playing field with the same life chances as others. In the winter of 2005 I was working in my capacity as an addictions worker in one of the Scottish Prisons. It was 7.30am and due to personal circumstances, I was in the lowest place that I had ever been in my life and could see no way out. Something was missing.

Someone had given me a book called *Nobody's Child* by a guy called John Robinson. It was about a boy (John) who came from a broken family, was a Bernardo's boy, and ended up in prison. Whilst there, he came to know Jesus and gave his life to Him. I was a real cynic at that time, but there was a phone number at the end of the book and a footnote saying, if you want to know more about Jesus or John, phone the number ... so I did. To my surprise, John answered the phone. I told him my story and where I was at. He asked what I did for a living and I told him. He said, "That's what I do too!" Coincidence right? Wrong. God-incidence! John advised me to find a local Alpha Course, go along and ask as many stupid or difficult questions as I wanted, and if I was still not convinced, to phone him back.

I went along to Greenview Evangelical Church in Glasgow and met two of the most patient men I have ever known: Ian McDonald and Andy Hunter. They listened to all my ranting and raving and answered all of my questions as best they could. It's embarrassing now to think that one of the questions I asked was, "If I become a Christian, can I still wear jeans?" I was serious. The image I had of Christians at that time was thick lensed glasses, corduroy trousers and big woolly jumpers – and that was just the women!

After a few weeks of their incredible patience and kind hospitality and, of course, input from Nicky Gumbel, I decided to give my life to Jesus.

I did not have that flashing light Damascus Road experience that some have, but I knew deep within that something had changed.

I suddenly felt that I really belonged and was finally accepted as "me". This was a real first for me. It was the first time I'd had a real father. I still struggle with that relationship at times, but that's my fault as I'm just not used to that son and Dad thing.

Being a Christian is not an easy road, so dont let anyone tell you it is, but it is the most exciting and rewarding road you can take. I now have a Father who is with me always, will never let me down and who really loves me – and I have learned to love and respect others. I still keep in touch with John and he continues to do amazing work for God all over the world.

Back to the music... At the same time that I became a Christian I began writing songs. I liked lyrics and had written loads over a period of years. I was greatly influenced by the great songwriting storytellers, such as Lennon and McCartney, Bruce Springsteen, Jackson Browne, Billy Joel, Crosby, Stills and Nash and The Eagles. But there were and are many, many more.

As I only played drums (and pipes!) which are not ideal for writing songs, I decided to learn guitar and ten years later I am a wee bit better, but not much. Let's just say I play guitar like a drummer!

My first album, *Cold and Roofless*, was a miracle. A good friend of mine Fraser Speirs agreed to produce it for me. Fraser is a virtuoso blues harp/harmonica player and he has worked with Muddy Waters, Van Morrison, James Taylor, Paulo Nuttini and many others. I was honoured that he had agreed to do this and he asked if he could involve a friend of his and use his friend's recording studio. His friend was none other than Graeme Duffin of Wet, Wet, Wet, an outstanding musician, producer, engineer and a Christian as well.

The problem was, where would I find the money to fund such a project? Although the album proceeds were going to homeless charities like the Glasgow City Mission, I could not get anyone interested in funding it. Then in stepped God and a chance meeting with a local church minister, who offered to fund the project but wished to remain anonymous. He has also kept me onside over a number of years. Cheers Ref!

The album was released and sold well at gigs and still does. The standard and quality of the production and playing that Fraser and Graeme provided on that first album is second to none. But I've noticed that it's the lyrics that have made the biggest impact on people over the years. *Cold and Roofless*, apart from being an obvious play on words, makes reference to the number of roofless people in our cities. There are homeless people who, although they have no home, are able to have a roof over their heads in maybe a hostel or on a friend's couch. But roofless people have nothing. They sleep under bridges, in doorways or under cardboard and that saddens me.

My next album, *Faith to Faith*, also came about by a chance meeting with (now close friend) Davy Jones. Davy is an incredibly talented musician, singer, producer, motivator and a very kind Christian man. He had just opened his own recording studio (Davy Jones Locker). We talked and Davy offered to record an album with me for free. I couldn't believe it and the result (12 long months later!) is the album which is *Faith to Faith*. This title is also a play on words (no, I don't have a lisp!). It refers to my change from Judaism to Christianity and how God has changed my life. It also includes songs that relate to my wonderful and beautiful wife and family (thank you for your patience) and, of course, my struggles and the struggles too many face in this world of ours. Since the release of this album, many people have asked me about the lyrics and told me how different songs affected them and how much they meant to them.

Soon after the release of this album I was asked if I would perform at a series of gigs and events and I had to put together a band relatively quickly to meet this demand. *The Hope Street Band* was born. The name came from yet another play on words. Hope Street is one of the main streets in Glasgow and "Hope Street" is where I wanted to see people end up: on a street with hope and a future. Of course, as a huge fan of Bruce Springsteen, I kind of borrowed and adapted the name from the *E Street Band*. Sorry Bruce!

The *Meet Me at The Cross* album was completely God led. I had some rough ideas and melodies for ten new songs, but as I had never written or had any inclination to write "Christian" or "praise songs" I had not planned that they would turn out the way they did. But once again, "God had other plans for me." He also brought across my path an incredibly gifted and talented musician and record producer Sam (Samuel) Gallagher who is an absolute genius to work with. Sam's work ethic, ability and gentle nature make his studio (EssGee Productions based in Barrhead Glasgow), the best experience that any musician/writer could ever want. God bless all you do Sam!

Over the years, many people asked me why I'd never published the lyrics as a stand alone project. They (kindly) told me how the words touched them, made them cry, made them laugh and comforted them during difficult times in their lives. I am humbled to know this and to know that my words (or the words that God has given me), have had such a positive impact on people's lives.

I thank God for this ability and for the opportunities that He has provided to share this talent. I thank Him also for the many people He has brought across my path, who have given so much of their time, expertise, patience and kindness to help me on my journey. There are far too many to mention, but I single out my wife, my mum, my family, Davy Jones, Archie Dickson, David Barron, and all my other close friends who have been there through thick and thin. To everyone who had faith in me (and you know who you are) I thank you from the bottom of my heart. To everyone who had no faith in me (and you know who you are too!) I also thank you from the bottom of my heart for making me even more determined.

I suppose, therefore, that this book took me ten years to write, as the lyrics first appeared ten years ago on *Cold and Roofless*. But then I suppose it really took me over 50 years, since the stories on that first recording were stories based on my life and the lives of others I had known directly or indirectly over my lifetime.

There have been many "scars and stripes" in my life, which have either been self inflicted, inflicted by others, or sadly, inflicted upon others by me. The purpose of this book, the lyrics and the stories behind the lyrics, is to raise awareness of the various issues that affect people socially, personally, mentally, physically and spiritually, and to hopefully change lives for the better. To help others find love, hope and faith and ultimately to point them towards Jesus Christ. Or at the very least, plant a seed of interest that makes someone want to know more and ask questions before making a life changing decision, either way.

I hope that this book and these lyrics and stories help start you on your own journey and encourage you to ask your own questions. If you need someone to walk with, just ask and He will walk with you as He walks with me. There are links at the back of this book that may help with that journey, but the first step starts with you.

God bless,
Michael

If you wish to contact Michael, book him for a speaking engagement, or book Michael with The Hope Street Band for a music event, please use the following Email address: 999mikmak@gmail.com

Part One
From the Heart of the Streets

everything
tastes good
when you're
hungry

[Michael McMillan © 2007 from the album
Cold and Roofless available on iTunes]

I was working in HMP Barlinnie in Glasgow as an addictions worker, when I overheard two "residents" in conversation. One was new to the resort and was complaining loudly about the food (which actually wasn't that bad). His roommate said, "Son, when you are truly hungry, everything tastes good."

While walking through the town I saw a young man lift a discarded chip packet that someone had thrown away and eat the remains. It really got me thinking that in the United Kingdom we are really not that united. We don't realise just how well off some of us are, and how we take many things for granted - things that could be taken away in an instant, such as dignity, freedom, health, friends, family, children, job, wealth and life itself.

I missed the last bus from the city, it was cold and I started to roam
And it seemed such a terrible pity for the people who thought it was home
The drunks on the corner were shouting at women with no self-respect
And a child of fourteen just should not have been the victim of so
much neglect

Everything tastes good when you're hungry,
You'll sing almost anyone's song
You'll eat pain and hurt and you'll swallow the dirt
When you ain't tasted love for so long

A man lording over his lady, there is not a hair out of place,
She cowers in fear as he wipes off a tear, then I noticed that bruise on her face
A young boy, his eyes filled with sorrow, eats food that's been thrown on
the street and then he gets in a car with the man from the bar who pays
him just to be sweet

Everything tastes good when you're hungry,
You'll sing almost anyone's song
You'll eat pain and hurt and you'll swallow the dirt
When you ain't tasted love for so long

It's not what you do that's important, it's what you could do but don't that's
the cause
So when you're stuck on a course that would choke any horse remember
hunger is still the best sauce
And when you're sitting at home with your loved ones, don't you judge the
young girl on the street
Or the man with no hope who's just trying to cope without any shoes on
his feet

Everything tastes good when you're hungry,
You'll sing almost anyone's song
You'll eat pain and hurt and you'll swallow the dirt
When you ain't tasted love for so long

life

[Michael McMillan © 2007 from the album
Cold and Roofless available on iTunes]

It's a hard life when you are born on the wrong side of the tracks. When you live in a dog-eat-dog society that neither wants you there, nor throws you a crust to get by. All too often people are forced to do what they need to do just to survive and to be able to put food on the table for their families and their children.

"Maurice" was one such man. I met him when he was on a home visit not long before he was finally released. Despite the hardness and obvious mistrust he had developed over the years, he let his guard down just once in my company when his children arrived and it was then that I saw a love, gentleness and kindness in him I had never seen before. I knew then that this man did have a future and that this son would rise again.

In sixty six a boy arrived
And Sally Murray cried with pride
His sister Sarah cried herself to sleep

A lonely girl with a lonely life
She'd make someone a lonely wife
For now there was another mouth to feed

In the darkness she lay staring at the moonlight on the trees
And her sadness kept her praying for someone to set her free

The boy soon grew into a man and he walked the path where the
Bad men ran, his family never starved another day,
For life is hard when you have no choice and harder still when you
have no voice, and no one really cares much anyway

She got married to a stranger that she'd known all of her life
He was cold and he was danger, now a prisoner as his wife

In ninety three a shot rang loud and Sally's heart was not so proud
She called her son and saw it in his eyes
Though Morris Murray's time was out he'd left his enemies in no doubt
To steal from this man really wasn't wise

She had children and she left him, studied hard now and changed her life
But the world she thought she wanted was full of horror, sin and vice

Ten years gone and the seasons change her setting son will rise again
And Sally Murray prays for days to come
And Morris in his prison cell prays to heaven from this hell
And asks forgiveness for the things he's done

The winds of autumn brought an angel and he loved her then she knew
All the others had betrayed her but this angel had been true

in
his
eyes

[Michael McMillan © 2010 from the album
Faith to Faith available on iTunes]

In his eyes came about when I met a man who had served many a long sentence in prison for crimes of violence. Although I no longer agree with a "tooth for a tooth and an eye for an eye" way of life, I can understand that many people are forced to live this way in order to survive.

As a young man in a gang-filled area of Glasgow, "David" and his brother had to be tougher, harder and faster than the next person in order to carve out a living. Glasgow was rife with gangs and gang warfare, and most young men (and some young women) carried a knife or a razor blade and were not afraid to use it. The Police at that time were, and had to be, an authoritarian force and David and young people like him regarded them as the enemy.

Sadly, that's the world they lived in – a world most people don't understand and why should they? *"For life is hard when you have no choice and harder still when you have no voice, and no one really cares much anyway."*

However, in spite of his upbringing, "David" finally gave his life to Jesus Christ and now he is one of the most respected (and still the hardest!), well thought of men in his community. He has been a real inspiration to many young men in the area, the same area he grew up in, and he has been a real inspiration to me. Thank you brother.

I met a man last Friday, a killer I'd been told,
They said that he was troubled by the stories he'd been sold.
We talked about the future and when the conversation died,
I could see a kindness in his eyes

He had the face of city thunder and a hurting deep inside,
A lost and wounded lion still searching for his pride.
He said the city's just a prison with a different kind of bars.
He saw the moon but only reached the scars

He said I hope that they will leave me to live my life in peace.
It's all that I can hope for when I finally find release,
And I know it won't be easy trying to start my life again,
But I hope I find a true love who can help me with the pain

He said you buy into the system where the system lets you dwell,
So he bought a chunk of hardness, the kind that prisons sell
And he said that she'd been faithful as fifteen years went by,
But I could see a sadness in his eyes

He had a reputation that even I had heard,
He could disturb the comfortable and comfort the disturbed,
But deep inside this fighting man I had met the wise
And I could see a Son rise in his eyes

When we finished talking he shook me by the hand,
He said you didn't judge me and I know you understand
What's past is past and what's ahead is way too far to see,
What matters most is what's inside of me

I met a man last Friday, a killer I'd been told,
I could see that he was troubled by the lies that he'd been sold,
But when we talked about his children I saw the love inside
And I could see a future in his eyes

the
other
half

[Michael McMillan © 2008 from the album
Faith to Faith available on iTunes]

This one started off as a play on words. I wrote down many lines and phrases that had the word "half" in them. But when I started pulling them together a story emerged which I clearly recognised: people who start something half heartedly that they never finish. This could be a course, a diet, fitness regime or a commitment to a relationship, person, family or their faith. They look back and tell anyone who will listen that their lives have been so unlucky and that everyone else is to blame, but really they did not commit themselves and only gave it 50% ... or half!

I really like this wee song. In Glasgow "a half" is well known as a half pint of beer or a whisky – usually both. Men will order their first half and a half, and lose half the day (with their newly found "half brother") and a whole lot more!

In the half light of the evening from a half moon in the sky,
there's a half cut man just sitting watching half his life go by
and he never could remember was he half right or half wrong,
as half the things he started failed when half time came along

Half the time, half the picture the other half is out of reach,
like photographs torn in half
and you only have half each

You share half your life with someone who is always half asleep
and when your half gone with your half pint then you're in the half that's
deep and your newly found half brother talks you in to half a day
then you end the night half crazy because you've only got half pay

Half the time, half the picture the other half is out of reach, like
photographs torn in half and you only have half each

Half a love he needed so just learned half the dance
but when this half fool was half empty he just wanted half a chance,
but in half an hour his half love will be half a world away
and he thought for half a second that half her heart would stay

Half the time, half the picture the other half is out of reach, like
photographs torn in half and you only have half each

unwanted

[Michael McMillan © 2008 from the album
Faith to Faith available on iTunes]

I often walk down Byres Road in Glasgow's West End and it really highlights how socially divided my city is. I met a man called Michael who begged on the streets. I know his story and will neither share it nor judge him. I had seen and met many men like him in my job as an addictions counsellor and as a volunteer at The Glasgow City Mission (there by the grace of God go I).

Michael sits on the pavement in all weathers and in all conditions. Over time we struck up a kind of mutual trust. I would never insult him by saying it was a friendship, because it could never be that. But I always wondered how he saw the world and one day I asked him.

The thing that struck him most, and hurt him most, was the total lack of love and care people had for each other as they rushed to spend money they could ill afford to spend. He became un-noticed and felt unwanted. He could clearly see the people who, before long, could or would be in the same situation as him. From the pavement looking up he could see the sin rise.

"Too many people spend money they don't have on things they don't need to impress people they don't like." I have been one of those people at times in my life and I am sure you have too.

Even the city has its
seasons, in autumn
people turn to grey.

Through lonely summers
some are lonely, then
winter winds blow them
away

Like leaves that gather
uninvited, from down
below he looks above,
he could see the way
they lived life, he just
wondered if they loved.

He had learned his lesson early that poverty begins at home
Methadone was in his madness as he wandered all alone

Looking at unwanted posters of unwanted souls,
Unwanted lovers playing unwanted roles,
Unwanted hate, unwanted pain,
Unwanted children, unwanted again

For every man there is in prison, there are others doing the time,
Mothers, fathers, sisters, lovers with children living on the line
Don't you know this is our country, you boast about its reputation,
But the way you treat each other, it's an un-united nation.
It's a diminishing republic. not for poor or sick or old,
Or the young who are downtrodden, or those left out in the cold

Looking at unwanted posters of unwanted souls,
Unwanted lovers playing unwanted roles,
Unwanted hate, unwanted pain,
Unwanted children, unwanted again

the
city
mission

[Michael McMillan © 2013 from the album
Meet Me at the Cross available on iTunes]

Having been a musician, a police officer, an addictions worker in prisons and in the community, and a volunteer at Glasgow City Mission, I have seen a side of life that many people will thankfully never see. This song was inspired by the people who live on the streets of Glasgow and every other city in this place we call the United Kingdom or Great Britain. I have no political or religious leaning, I am a Christian and it makes me very sad to see the way we treat each other and how this world of ours could be the beautiful wonderful place that God created if we would just "care". It's as simple as that people.

Instead of rushing across the world for some cause or another, if you really want this world to have love and to share love, one with another, start small, start in your own home, start with your own family, start in your own street, start in your own village or town, start in your own workplace, or maybe you need to start in your own church.

Would you welcome the addict, prostitute, homeless man, woman or child into your church? Would you sit beside them? Would you feed them? How many of you church-going people have no friends, no neighbours, no work colleagues? Nobody, eh! So when was the last time you invited them to church? I (sadly) saw a sign which read "More and more people are moving away from the church and moving closer to God." Is that your church? (Hebrews 13:2)

Standing on the edge of darkness I could see your face
Waiting once again to see the sin rise
There's a mission in this city you said it couldn't wait
Make a move before another soul dies

And on that day when I stood with you
I knew we did the best we could,
Nothing more that any man could do
They didn't fall because of how we stood

Rushing out across the world looking for a cause
When the cause is standing right in front of you
People dying, children crying, men profit from their loss
Don't stand and watch as time runs out on you

And on that day when I stood with you
I knew we did the best we could,
Nothing more that any man could do
They didn't fall because of how we stood

They were rising sons
Now they are setting sons
They are someone's sons
Will they ever see The Son?

Blessed are the peacemakers we are called the sons of God
Silently we wait to see the sin rise
Another mission in another city we know that it can't wait
We will fight before another soul dies

And on that day when we stood with you
We knew we did the best we could
Nothing more that any man could do
They didn't fall because of how we stood

sticks
and
stones

[Michael McMillan © 2010 from the album
Faith to Faith available on iTunes]

The first lie I was ever told was that "sticks and stones will break my bones but words will never hurt me". Lies all lies. This is a song about infidelity, lies and other domestic issues. For all the young people (and not so young) reading this, never judge lovers by good looking covers! The cover always fades before the content.

Despair can lead to a very dark place, but there is nothing, nothing in this world worth taking your life for: no boyfriend, no girlfriend, no job, no exam result, no bill, no look, no fashion, no whatever. I lost my father and some close friends through suicide and when you look into each case, there was always a way out, an alternative to taking that life. You must speak with someone, anyone you can truly trust. If you can't speak with your family, parents, partner, loved one, then find someone, anyone, but don't you dare give up. Pray, speak to Him. He WILL listen and He WILL help you.

Well she thought about the night they met the fruit without the passion
The local heart throb, tough and lean, the look, the build, the fashion
Well he lied to her again that night, betrayal, tears, excuses
A strange new perfume filled the air and pain that leaves no bruises

And she said baby please be careful whenever we're apart
Sticks and stones will break my bones but your words break my heart

He thought that he could read her right and get inside her head,
but she could read between the lies and hear what wasn't said
But when the chips are down we fish around for excuses in the dark
Never getting down to the heart of the matter or the matters of the heart

He wondered what was behind her fronts, but she could hear him thinking,
He spent his whole life floating around while her broken heart was sinking

And she said baby please be careful whenever we're apart
Sticks and stones will break my bones but your words break my heart
And baby please remember every time you start
Sticks and stones will break my bones but your words break my heart

what
can you
do

[Michael McMillan © 2007 from the album
Cold and Roofless available on iTunes]

This is about infidelity, hypocrisy, lies, deceit and making right and wrong choices. Many people impose their values and beliefs on others and insist that they adhere to them and abide by them ... and then live a completely different way themselves.

If you are in a difficult, abusive, relationship with someone who allows you to "live by their leave", get out, run as fast as you can and "when you leave, you can live."

When the spirit (whisky) slips away, or your spirit (strength) is slipping away, and you have given up the ghost; when you are in a place that even angels fear to tread and the shoe is on the other foot ... what will you do?

Was this something he should have dealt with,
Was there something hidden going down?
Though the past fades away will the memories stay
As Sodom and Gomorrah hit this town
She caused him heartbreak but he endured it
Because he loved her he would wear this thorny crown
Now he was paying the price for the sin and the vice
And for all the other men that let her down

What can you do when the ghost gives up on you what can you say when
Your spirit slips away, what do you hear when your angel treads your fear,
What can you do when her foot is on another's shoe

She always said she wanted honesty,
Straight, on ice with no lies,
But he knew that she drank on those honesty nights
From the well she said she despised.
Now the tactics that she was teaching
Was not the practice she was preaching
And her endless hope faced a hopeless end
With the letters her heart forgot to send

What can you do when the ghost gives up on you what can you say when
Your spirit slips away, what do you hear when your angel treads your fear,
What can you do when her foot is on another's shoe

He is looking for a road now it's the one he should have taken at the start
And he knows if he stays it's a very long way on that journey from her
head back to her heart

What can you do when the ghost gives up on you what can you say when
Your spirit slips away, what do you hear when your angel treads your fear,
What can you do when her foot is on another's shoe

the
only
word

[Michael McMillan © 2007 from the album
Cold and Roofless available on iTunes]

I ran away from home when I was very young and ended up in London.
I was (and still am) a drummer and met and played with many people,
famous and infamous. I got involved in many things and did many things
that I shouldn't have ... and to excess. I lost a lot of good friends through
drink, drugs and fighting and I lost my first real love.

I kept running and running, until I realised that it was me that I
couldn't get away from. I was fragile and close to the edge when I felt His
hand reaching out to me. At that time I didn't know who He was, but I sure
do now.

I hit the road when I was seventeen
It didn't matter what they said
I'd find someone who believed in me
We'd live the dreams inside my head.
But I soon found that world was cold
That the rainbow's end was the rich man's gold
And I thought love was the only word
But I found love to be a lonely word.

I tried to be the man they asked of me
The one my mother thinks I am
I wanted love I wanted dignity
I need to be a needed man
But I soon found though I was running free
That I kept running just to get away from me
And I thought love was the only word
But I found love to be a lonely word.

Too many years that passed have not been kind,
So many lines upon my face
I talked the talk and walked the walk for them,
But I was never in their race,
I was on that ledge thinking what will be will be
And then I felt your hand reaching out to me
When I thought love was a lonely word
You showed me love ... is the only word.

the ballad
of
Mickey Silver

[Michael McMillan © 2008 from the album
Faith to Faith available on iTunes]

My father's name was Mickey. In my teenage years and throughout my life I have seen and been involved in many deaths, often caused through revenge. It must stem from my childhood that I just hate seeing anyone being bullied, abused or mistreated and, as an adult, I can do something about that ... and did on many occasions. Or maybe I just watched too many cowboy films when I was younger!

I can't say much more. You can make your own mind up about this one. Enough said...

It was six thirty in the morning twenty second day of May
The town folk were all gathered, a man would hang today
Mickey had always been a loner, since the war had brought him here
Tough and hard and battle scarred they would never see his tears

Won't you tell them Mickey Silver, won't you tell them of your pain
Won't you tell them Mickey Silver, tell them all her precious name
Won't you tell them how she held you
How she calmed the rage inside
As you take that final step to your lover's side

Well she had always been a strong one, but was pure as driven snow
She took the word of Jesus where the angels feared to go
But some men are not for telling and some men want much more
Her screams had died to silence when Mickey walked in through that door

He could see their leering faces and the deed that they had done
He watched it turn to horror when the flames came from his guns
The silent night was shattered Satan's bell began to ring
Through the sound of distant thunder he heard his angel sing

Can you hear me Mickey Silver, can you feel me standing near
Don't be frightened Mickey Silver, I will take away your fear
Standing side by side forever in a land beyond the sky
Where we will never hear the sound of another's cry

The gallows are still standing and the town folk still recall
The smile on Mickey Silver's face when he took that final fall
Many years have passed un-noticed, winters melting into spring
And if you listen very closely you can still hear Mickey sing

Don't you cry for Mickey Silver, don't you cry for me you hear
Don't you cry for Mickey Silver, don't you cry a single tear
Don't you cry for me tomorrow, don't you cry to God above
For tonight I'm in the arms of the one I love.

**Part Two
From the Streets of the Heart**

your treasure
is where your
heart is

[Michael McMillan © 2013 from the album
Meet Me At The Cross available on iTunes]

I co-wrote this song with a good friend, Alan Campbell. Alan is a very gifted musician and songwriter in his own right and he came up with the wonderful melody which I altered slightly and put the lyrics to it. I was visiting Alan in London and during that visit his children came over. Alan's strong love for his family and children (and grandchildren) was so evident that it got me thinking about my own children and how precious they are to me. I love my children very much and I tell them as often as I can, even when it embarrasses them (sorry son!) As parents we often spend too much time trying to give our children all the things that we did not have, instead of the things we do have ... our love and our time. Don't waste another second, tell them how much you love them right now any way you can, but tell them ... and make sure they know it. This is for all parents of children everywhere.

Children's laughter and it seems like yesterday
With eyes that sparkle, you had so very much to say
On the day that you were born my world turned upside down
Tears of joy, you know I thought that I might drown

Your treasure is where your heart is
And the heart is always true
No matter where I go my child,
My heart stays there with you

So much beauty little girl God gave to you
With a heart that matches everything you say and do
Strength and courage, son you make me feel so proud
But with love and kindness that make you stand out from the crowd

Your treasure is where your heart is
And the heart is always true
No matter where I go my child,
My heart stays there with you

Take good care of your mother when the dark clouds come her way
Love your sister love your brother
And you'll bring light to my day

Time soon passes and you are out there on your own
Make your own mistakes raise a family, build a home
But please remember what I have been trying to say
Tell your children that you love them every day

Because your treasure is where your heart is
And the heart is always true
No matter where I go my child,
My heart stays there with you

wait
for
me

[Michael McMillan © 2008 from the album
Faith to Faith available on iTunes]

It's very difficult to carry on when a loved one leaves us. The friends who drift back to their own lives, the awkward silences in company, and when we are alone. A smell, a song or just a word that reminds us of another time and place. That secret island we long to be on again. Except we would be alone this time ... or would we?

There is another life after death. I know that's a huge statement, but it's based on faith. I believe that Jesus Christ is the Son of the Living God, that He died on that cross and three days later was resurrected. I have asked His forgiveness for all my sins and I am forgiven. If He can do it for me, He can do it for you. Just ask and accept and see the change in your life.

If you ask Him into your life and I'm wrong, then you will have lost nothing. But If you don't ask Him into your life and I was right, then you will have lost everything!

If I should leave this world before you
Promise me we will never part
For all the times I held you
And all the love you brought to my heart

The light above the crystal water
The bright reflection of your smile
Upon our secret island
Standing side by side for a while

The love we have we take for granted
Until the one we love has gone
Though our hearts are heavy
Somehow we find the strength to go on

When you call and no one answers
When the silence makes you cry
Too late to say I'm sorry
Far too late to say goodbye

Like a ship out on the water, at the mercy of the sea
Like a lamb led to the slaughter, I just wander aimlessly
Through the days I hear your laughter it's at night I go insane
No more happy ever afters, until I'm holding you again

Beneath the warm Havana sunset
Blood red sun cries on the sea
There I'll call your name out
And I will know that you are with me

But if you leave this world before me
Know that I will never rest
Until it's time for me
And I can feel your head on my chest

song
for
alex

[Michael McMillan © 2008 from the album
Faith to Faith available on iTunes]

Matthew 9:18-22 – I have read this passage of Scripture many times in the past and previously saw/read it for nothing more than it was: two more miracles that Jesus performed. The woman had been bleeding for many years and was instantly cured and the young girl was dead and was miraculously brought back to life by Jesus.

My own life and marriage took a real turn for the worse a couple of years ago. It involved many factors and people, in one way or another, in what was to become a bit of a circus sideshow. Isn't it amazing what (and who) crawls out of the woodwork or from beneath a stone when things are going wrong?

Sadly, some people seem to thrive on other's misfortune; it seems to fill a void in their own lives and give them a "project" to work on for a short while, anyway. I was amazed and disappointed (but not surprised) how some people did not wish us well when God changed our hearts and, in so doing, changed the whole situation and resurrected our marriage.

But back to the scripture. To anyone out there who is struggling with any situation that seems unfixable: keep praying and keep believing. No matter how long the problem has been going on, no matter how dead the situation seems to be, it's not over until He says it's over and it's not dead until He says it's dead. As for my wife, well she's just the best and I love her so very much xx. Thank you, Father

If it wasn't for the fact
that I don't have any money
I'd buy the world
and give it all to you
I know that you still find
that kind of funny
But deep within my heart
I always knew
That every time I tried
to stop these feelings
I know your heart is
calling out my name
You take away the pain
and start the healing
And lead me from
my anger and my pain

And then you tell me that you love me
And I can feel it in your kiss
And I can tell the way you hold so tight
That you need a love like this

I knew it from the moment that I saw you,
The hunger and the sorrow in your eyes
You took my heart as if it was part of you,
It helped you find the truth beyond the lies
So many times you told me that you need me
And how you never felt this way before,
But every time you left my heart was bleeding
This angel needs to love you so much more.

But then you tell me that you love me
And I can feel it in your kiss
And I can tell the way you hold so tight
That you need a love like this

To be still is what He taught me,
Like the dust upon the shelf
And I thank The Lord you caught me,
And you saved me from myself

41

dreams

[Michael McMillan © 2008 from the album
Cold and Roofless available on iTunes]

I wrote this song lyric when I was in a really dark place. I could see many of the old faces, my friends and associates, "fading away" in one way or another. Like my jeans, my close friends were fading fast through drink and drugs and violence and from just believing the lie that they no longer had a purpose or a future, or anything to give or live for.

I started thinking that there must be more to life than this. I could not believe that as a musician, songwriter and writer I had not seen it before: that behind every book, poem, song, work of art or creation, there must be an artist ...or a creator.... and there is, so I started telling them!

In my dreams I make appointments that in life I cannot keep
But I have to be a dreamer because at night I cannot sleep
It can't be wrong to be a dreamer if I share my dreams with you
Now I know you will make my dreams come true

Scared of heartache, fear of failure, never knowing what to do
I talked to strangers, hidden dangers when I should have talked to you
You turned the madness into gladness made me see what true love means
As you helped me realise my dreams

And if my dreams, all my dreams of pipes and glens
If they should turn, turn to pipe dreams once again
Would you stay and be with me on that day
All my blue jean friends fade away?

Across the troubled seas of sadness I have struggled to your shore
Like a bird above the water I will fly forever more
Faith and courage, pain and anger, have all put me to the test
Take my hand and God will do the rest

And if my dreams, all my dreams of pipes and glens
If they should turn, turn to pipe dreams once again
Would you stay and be with me on that day
All my blue jean friends fade away?

you
are

[Michael McMillan © 2008 from the album
Faith to Faith available on iTunes]

What can I tell you? This is obviously about the most beautiful woman in the world!!!

You are so beautiful
You are a love so fine, a love divine
You are my daily sunlight
You are my only moonlight
You smile my darkness into light
Your laughter brightens up my day

You are a special place
You are a precious grace
Nearer clearer
You take my hand you understand
You are the stars in my sky
You are my strength when I cry
You lift me high above the clouds
I want to shout your name out loud

You are so magical
You are so wonderful
Sweet face, sweet grace
I watch you sleep in love so deep
And each morning when you rise
The sky takes blue from your eyes
The flowers call your name out loud
You make me feel so very proud

You are

song
for my
children

[Michael McMillan © 2007 from the album
Cold and Roofless available on iTunes]

I love them so much. In the past I hurt them and God only knows the damage that I did at that time. But in spite of me, they have grown into wonderful, beautiful, loving, caring people and we are good now. They are amazing and I love them so much.

So many times how I wish
I had told you
All the things that
I kept in my heart
How I love you when
You're with me
How I love you
When we are apart

Trying hard to achieve
What we can't do
We are forced into doing
What we can

Please forgive me if I'm not perfect
I have made mistakes, I'm just a man

For some day you will find a love of your own
And I pray that you are true to your heart
And you both reach that goal that's deep in your soul
On the road that we shared at the start

Don't believe all you hear, make your own mind
Trust the wisdom and innocence of youth
There are three sides to each story
What you see, what you hear and the truth

Don't forget but forgive, it's not easy
And in time we will make a new start
In my dreams I will hold you, in my soul and in my heart

For some day you will find a love of your own
And I pray that you are true to your heart
And you both reach that goal that's deep in your soul
On the road that we shared at the start

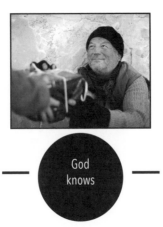

God
knows

[Michael McMillan © 2008 from the album
Faith to Faith available on iTunes]

I had a really messed up, mixed up childhood. My father committed suicide. I was in a religion I didn't know and that didn't want to know me. I fought with everyone. I was an angry young man and grew up very bitter inside about life in general, but especially about adults who I couldn't trust, who told me one thing and did another, who lived one way and told me to live another way, who were never there for me, who let me down, who lied to me and deceived me...who I couldn't trust. But then I met someone at a "bus stop" along the road and all that changed...

I was very pleased to be there when those thoughts came back to me
I was happy to be anywhere, happy just to be
I was sick and tired of hearing the liars and the just
Sick and tired of feeling that I could never trust
Then I saw you standing, smiling and my heart just took control
I told you of my many lives and bared my very soul
And you listened to my stories and you said you'd be my friend
But I prayed that you would stay when the stories end

And I thank God you love me, in my darkness you are there
In your eyes I see a future, when you smile I know you care
In the barren wastelands of my heart the seed of your love grows
How your love has found me? God knows

I told you that I'd lost someone, the pain was clear to see
A person died so long ago that person's name was me
And I said I'd been a fighter and a killer to my shame
But if I'd killed that man inside my head, to God that's just the same
For you see by crying wolf somehow I hoped a wolf would come
And then I could save you from it and be a hero to someone
And you listened to my stories and you swore you'd be my friend
But I pray that you will stay when the stories end

And I thank God you love me, in my darkness you are there
In your eyes I see a future, when you smile I know you care
In the barren wastelands of my heart the seed of your love grows
How your love has found me? God knows

tell
me

[Michael McMillan © 2007 from the album
Cold and Roofless available on iTunes]

Sometimes you just can't do right for doing wrong and no matter how hard you try, for some people it will never be good enough. When I wrote this I had had my fill of those kinds of people. It really wears you down being constantly told that you are not good enough, that you will never be good enough and that you will never amount to anything. Don't believe that lie. Remove yourself from all of those people and surround yourself with people who genuinely care about you and have a positive influence in your life. Be the "you" He made you to be.

I heard a wise man say, "preach the gospel and if you have to ... use words." I like that. Live your life in such a way that people can see and feel the goodness, kindness and love that is inside you, pouring from the things you say and do.

I could never write a love song that would show you how I feel
For how could I write passion and make it warm and real

I sing you songs of others when I feel the need to try
But if I should write a love song it would only make you cry

So tell me how you're feeling
Show me how you care
Tell me how you're feeling
Now I'm not there

I never saw it coming, you took me by surprise
I was captured by your beauty and the sadness in your eyes

You thought I had all the answers, you thought I'd played each part
But then you tore my world wide open and exploded in my heart

So tell me how you're feeling
Tell me that I'm wrong
Tell me how you're feeling
Now I'm gone

I wish that I could tell you in the words you want to hear
I know it's so important and it would take away your fear
But I could never write it, a song good enough for you

But can't you see it pouring from the things I say and do

walking
with
you

[Michael McMillan © 2013 from the album
Meet Me At The Cross available on iTunes]

I was walking along the beautiful shoreline at Tighnabruaich in Argyllshire at what was one of the worst times in my life, having separated from my wife. However, in spite of this, God carried me as He has done a hundred (1,000) times before. For the first time I was walking with Him and it felt just wonderful. No drink, no drugs, no nothing, just me, the Creator of the universe and this beautiful landscape He created.

How could I not be inspired to write this song with all that going on. The best corner men you can get when you're in a "real" fight are the Father, Son and Holy Ghost.

Of course, these lyrics could also refer to walking along this shoreline with a loved one, which I've also done!

New high walking along that road now
Not knowing where I will go now
But I'm walking along with you
Blue sky walking away from the past now
Watching it go so fast now as
I'm walking along with you

And in my heart I feel the love that you give to me
A brand new start, I'll be the man you made me to be

Sunshine like I've never felt before now
Walking along that shore now
Walking along with you
Sometimes when I'm talking to God above now
I think of the ones I love now
And pray they will walk with you

And in my heart I feel the love that you give to me
A brand new start I'll be the man you made me to be

Moonlight staring at all the stars now
Knowing I've come so far now
By walking along with you
Warm night I'm never going back to that cold road
I'm never going back to that old road
Because I'm walking along with you

And in my heart I feel the love that you give to me
A brand new start I'll be the man you made me to be

Part Three
Highway To Heaven

we
don't
listen

[Michael McMillan © 2007 from the album
Cold and Roofless available on iTunes]

If He did come back now (and when He does come back) will we be far too busy and focused on our own importance and with our own agendas that we won't even notice. I have met so many people through the years who are desperately looking for love, but they missed out on it because they were so busy with the trappings of this world that they did not recognise love when it came and sat down beside them ... before it moved on.

Isn't it funny how things turn out
We scream and shout
But we don't listen

There's no key to a broken lock
If we talk and talk
But we don't listen

Through the years and years of talking just imagine if you can
That the son of the Great Spirit reappeared again to man
And he tried so hard to show us how to fill our hearts with love
But as the wise and foolish talked and talked
He could not be heard above

Isn't it funny we begin to fear
When we don't hear
But we still don't listen
It doesn't matter who is right or wrong
We just can't go on
If we don't listen

And the righteous, well they might just start to listen to the choices
But if someone tells a different tale they would not hear those voices
And they ask us how we're doing with a cold and vacant stare
Because it's easier than telling us how little they could care
In the heat of thoughtless anger we don't see the risks we're taking
In our struggle for the last word we don't care whose hearts we're breaking
Saying after every battle that the last one was the last
But if history shows us one thing
There's no future in the past

Isn't it funny how things turn out
We scream and shout
But we don't listen
When love whispers in your ear
You won't hear if you don't listen

take
my
hand

[Michael McMillan © 2013 from the album
Meet Me At The Cross available on iTunes]

The entire *Meet Me At The Cross* album was God-breathed.

My close and dear friends David and Aileen Barron have a cottage in Tighnabruaich (pronounced tin-a-brew-ach) which they have allowed me to use over the years and where a lot of my music was written and developed.

I had all the melodies and a rough outline of the 10 songs that would make up this album. But for the first time ever, I felt God's hand in most of the lyrics that came out. This song, *Take My Hand,* came while I was in a very dark and broken place. On my knees I asked God to take my hand and lift me up. He did not let me down and never has. I then thought of other people who just need to know Him and to offer Him their hand. He'll take it and carry you until you can walk again.

Take his hand Lord for he is sinking
Take his hand Lord for he's been drinking
Tell him you'll never let him down
Show him you'll always be around
Take her hand Lord for she's been crying
Take her hand Lord for she's been dying
Tell her you'll always be around
Show her you'll never let her down

Lord they need to hear the truth somewhere
Lord they need to know that someone cares
To feel the love that's been denied
To know you'll be there when they cry

Take his hand Lord for he is wild now
Take his hand Lord he's just a child now
Tell him you'll never let him down
Show him you'll always be around
Take her hand Lord she needs love bad now
Take her hand Lord she's never had now
Tell her you'll never let her down
Show her you'll always be around

Lord they need to hear the truth somewhere
Lord they need to know that someone cares
To feel the love that's been denied
To know you'll be there when they cry

Take my hand Lord I want to know you
Take my hand Lord I need to show you
That I will never let you down
That I will always be around

Lord I need to hear the truth somewhere
Lord I need to know that someone cares
To feel the love that's been denied
To know you'll be there when I cry

WWJD

[Michael McMillan © 2013 from the album
Meet Me At The Cross available on iTunes]

Simply put, What Would Jesus Do? We make this life of ours too difficult, too complicated. We make our walk with God the same. If you believe that God is your father, and he is, know that he wants to have that father son/daughter relationship with you, based on love, care, trust, faith and a real future. It's not "man made" and has no limits. It's beyond anything you could imagine and it's very simple.

I wrote this song to cut through all the (word taken out that is not very Christian) the rubbish and to get straight to the heart of the matter (and the matter of the heart!) What Would Jesus do? Would He care what you wore, how you looked, what seat you had in church or what riches you'd managed to accumulate? Would He care who you knew or how connected you were, or what sins you'd committed. The answer is no, He wouldn't. He accepts you exactly where you are and as you are. Jesus says, come and follow me and your life will change. He does not say change your life and then come and follow me. Think about that. Come exactly as you are right now.

At times I struggle to be a good witness so I decided to get a large tattoo done on my forearm of a cross with the letters WWJD beneath it. The young lady doing the tattoo was very kind and chatted about life and the world in general. When we came to the letters she asked me what they stood for, so I told her. She thought about this for a while and I waited in anticipation. Then in a broad Glasgwegian accent she said, "Well, I'll tell ye what he widnae do. He widnae be getting a &*** tattoo!" Oh well, back to the drawing board!

If you think that life is hard on you
Take a look at what you've got
Stop complaining about the things you need
And think about what you just bought
See the poor man and the ragged child
A bitter pill is all they've tasted
A single mother crying in the dark
She could live on what you've wasted

But if you'll change these moments in your life
Then take the old road straight and true
But if you're lost meet me at the cross
And tell me what would Jesus do?

It doesn't matter who you used to be
Just remember who you are
Walk the walk but don't talk the talk
That you've been talking in that bar
Show example in your children's lives
Or regret will grab you by the throat
If you want to walk on the water
You better get out of that boat

And standing at the crossroads of your life
Take the old road straight and true
But if you're lost meet me at the cross
And tell me what would Jesus do?

And if by chance you should meet Him
Could you look him in the eye?
Could you tell him what you did today?
Could you explain the reason why?

And standing at the crossroads of your life
Take the old road straight and true
But if you're lost meet me at the cross
And tell me what would Jesus do?

don't
you
know

[Michael McMillan © 2013 from the album
Meet Me At The Cross available on iTunes]

I wrote this song for everyone who is walking through life alone or lonely –
and sometimes that can mean being alone in a crowd. People do not realise
that Jesus is walking right beside them and all they have to do is put their
hand out and ask Him into their lives. It's also about a soldier who has been
killed in battle and is now walking with Jesus, but his family do not realise
this and they are grieving for him. Don't you know? You do now!

Broken man why are you crying
Woman why are you crying
Don't you know that He's walking?
Don't you know that The Lord is walking next to you?

Little boy why are you crying
Little girl why are you crying
Don't you know that He's walking?
Don't you know that The Lord is walking next to you?

So lift your head up and see Him smiling
His open arms will hold you tight
There is no more shame he will carry your pain
And lead you by His light

Mama why are you crying
Papa why are you crying
Don't you know that He's walking?
Don't you know that The Lord is walking next to you?

Sister why are you crying
Brother why are you crying
Don't you know that He's walking?
Don't you know that The Lord is walking next to you?

And if you ask Him He will come in
And shine His light upon your face
Bring hope to your life and love you won't find
In any other place

Dear Lord stop their crying
Oh Lord stop their crying
Can't they see that you're walking?
Can't they see that The Lord is walking home with me?

this
love

[Michael McMillan © 2013 from the album
Meet Me At The Cross available on iTunes]

Again, a God-breathed lyric and I was so elated and excited when it came, but I also think that it speaks to many people about true love and about not wasting a moment when it comes calling. It should be treasured and never taken for granted. I have seen too many relationships ruined or left broken and unrepaired, simply by foolish pride and the inability to say sorry, to trust again and to get back up and keep fighting.

"Life's not about how hard you can hit ... it's about how hard you can be hit and still keep moving forward." (Rocky Balboa). We love you Rocky!

This love that you feel inside
(tell him that you love him)
You have never felt this before
And this love that you cannot hide
(tell him that you love him)
Love that burst straight through your door

Don't walk alone with you pride (tell him, tell him)
Don't walk away and let this true love be denied

This love is all you need
(you hear his voice within you)
Your heart wants to stay by his side
And this love is like the sea
(you feel the power lift you)
Love rising up like a tide

What can you lose, not a thing (go now, go now)
Take that first step and you will hear the angels sing

Feel this love that is waiting for you
Believe this love that is waiting for you
You need this love that is waiting for you
Receive this love that is waiting for you

This love is like the sun
(can you feel the heat inside you?)
Bringing that glow to your face
And this love is never done
(it will last forever)
Changing your heart with his grace

What can you lose, not a thing (go now, go now)
Take that first step and you will hear the angels sing

the
Lord's
waltz

[Michael McMillan © 2013 from the album
Meet Me At The Cross available on iTunes]

I just love this song and I am so blessed with finding the right lyric for it. I started writing this song a long, long time ago. I had the melody and worked on it over the years, but the words just never came. It was originally (humble apologies to all my English friends!) going to be the next Scottish National Anthem and I could just imagine thousands of Scottish fans at Hampden Park or Murrayfield singing it after beating our arch rivals soundly. Sadly, the results never came at either of these two great sporting arenas (or anywhere else!), but gladly God provided the lyric that did come.

It still brings a tear to my eye when I sing the last few lines at gigs and I pray that one day my children will come to know the Lord and ask him into their lives.

I have had people ask me if they can use these words at a loved one's funeral and I have been very humbled and honoured by this. I also hope that one day this song will be adopted by our armed forces personnel as an epitaph to fallen comrades.

I heard amazing grace
Before I knew your face
Long before I opened up that door
You saved a wretch like me
Showed me what I could be
And what I can't be any more
And now when I'm far from you
I'm not alone
I hear you calling me
Calling me home

What would you have me do?
Please can I walk with you?
No footstep alone in the sand
This father's love new to me
My anger subdued in me
The day that I reached for your hand
And here on these foreign fields with no star above
Your shield protecting me
Your grace and your love

Help me to be the man
Some people think I am
Give me the strength for this fight
Help me to hear your voice
Cut through the devil's noise
And I will bring souls to your light

But Lord there is one thing I would ask you to do
Look after my children and bring them back home to you
And when I'm in my autumn years
With no regrets and no more fears
I'll thank you for giving me that chance
For somewhere in heaven's halls a band plays a quiet waltz
Then you and I will have that last dance

the
quiet
man

[Michael McMillan © 2007 from the album
Cold and Roofless available on iTunes]

One of my favourite films of all time is *The Quiet Man,* starring John Wayne. When I came back from London, I worked for my Uncle Louis in his scrap metal business in Glasgow for a while. He was a gambler, a whisky drinker and a former boxer, a real character and my natural father's brother. Among other things, he called me the quiet man. Uncle Louis was a real character and he lived his life to the full, often to the detriment of his family and friends. But he taught me a lot about life and living and, in his own way, how to be a man – or what he thought a man should be like. At any given time throughout the day in the back shop of his scrap business, there could be some of Glasgow's most notorious gangsters and some of Glasgow's top Police officers ... happy days! But this song is not just about them, Uncle Louis or me, it's about Him.

They say it's the quiet ones you have to watch and I was pleased to read in the Bible that in spite of being equipped with the patience of all the angels, even He got angry at times ... so it's not just me!

He was a quiet man but from his love the people ran
And looking to the sky, he prayed that they would hear his cry
This was love so true and free that they hadn't known before
Flesh and blood for all to see that he hadn't shown before

When he was just a child, across the mountains cold and wild
The people asked his name and feared the reason why he came
It was a love that kept him strong and burned in him every night
And for this love they sang his song and held back the fear inside

But they knew, oh how they knew, it was over on that day
Blood and tears see their fears, see the wise men fade away
Quiet man now you can tell the one who guides your heart
Father son they are one and they will never be apart

He was a quiet man, in life and death doing the best he can
And through your storm-swept skies on darkest nights you'll hear his cries
Full of love that leads you on with light from the brightest star
In your heart he will be strong no matter where you are

He was a quiet man.

I
found
you

[Michael McMillan © 2007 from the album
Cold and Roofless available on iTunes]

So many people walk through this life blinkered. They are totally unaware of what they say and do and how their actions (or inactions) and words affect people in a positive or negative way. Over the years I have met many blinkered people who are quick to tell everyone how long they have "served". "I have been a Police officer for 20 years, so you don't need to tell me..." or "I have been a Christian for 20 years, so you don't need to tell me..." In reality, they have only served 1 year repeated 20 times. They have neither learned anything, nor could they teach anyone anything!

Some people die, but they carry on living
Sleepwalk in a world that's ready for giving

Been told so long they never should
Been told for years they never could
They start believing they're no good
Then I found you

Well I can't wait for a day that I love me
Walk through that gate with the warm sun above me

I've cheated hurt and I have lied
I am the reason that they cried
I wished a thousand times I'd died
Then I found you

I found you in the hills of home but I was young and proud
I found you on the backstreets where I screamed my fear out loud
I found you there on foreign fields in trenches cold with fear
You kept me safe, it gave me strength, knowing you were near

But in the end it's really me that I live with
I pour myself a daily dose of forgiveness
I walked across the bridge of sighs
I saw the love that's in your eyes
No more the man that I despise
Because I found you

faith
to
faith

[Michael McMillan © 2008 from the album
Faith to Faith available on iTunes]

I have walked many roads, gone from fight to fight and faith to faith, met many people I thought I could trust but couldn't, met many people I thought cared about me and loved me but didn't, met special people who did care for me and whom I could trust … but didn't realise it and wasted it. Then I met the One who did and does. The "scars and stripes" are still there, but there is a healing now and although I am still a work in progress, we are now fighting back to back and not faith to faith.

For many years I tried to sing my songs
I never knew where I was going wrong
I always thought that what would be would be
But God had other plans for me.

A young drum warrior with just one goal
Ages of rock had finally taken toll
But the rock of ages saved my soul
Atonement something new to me

And God alone my judge and jury now
No more pain and no more fury now
With you beside me I am stronger now
Back to back and faith to faith

So many people tried to tell me how
To live my life the way that they'd allow
Then I met three men that I trusted most
Father Son and Holy Ghost

I'm tired of travelling this lonely road
I'm tired of carrying this heavy load
I'm tired of trying to keep our dreams alive
Let me be still, let me arrive

And God alone my judge and jury now
No more pain and no more fury now
With you beside me I am stronger now
Back to back and faith to faith

[Michael McMillan © 2013 from the album
Meet Me At The Cross available on iTunes]

As a new Christian I used to take communion and not think about or really understand the symbolic meaning behind the bread and the wine. Then one day in Glasgow Elim Church I suddenly had an image of my own son taking that awful beating and being nailed in agony to that cross in my place, because of my sins, so that my sins could be forgiven. Then the penny finally dropped.

I struggled to get a lyric for this song and I kept putting it off and left it till last. I was going down a different road with it and it just wasn't happening. With only a couple of days left to finish it, I prayed and asked God to go for a walk with me. We walked from Tighnabruaich towards Portavadie and I asked Him to give me the lyrics to finish this song. When I got back to the cottage, the words just flowed. Thank you, Dad.

What can I say my Lord for all the things I've done?
You looked away my Lord the day you gave your only son
And in my darkest night not knowing what to do
I just remember you and the darkness you went through

I used to walk that road, where evil made its home
Lost on those city streets in a crowd, but all alone
Then I heard that calling somewhere inside my head
And I met an angel who said my life was dead

And when I turned away from darkness, I heard the angel say it's done
And then the shadows fell behind me as I turned to face your son
Then I understood the passion and I received his father's grace
I saw eyes of love and wisdom as I gazed upon his face

And when I take this bread I see his face so clear
The thorns upon his head, the blood, the pain, the tears
He is my only son and I can't turn away
Too big a sacrifice, my God what can I say?
But as I take this wine you clear the mist away
It was your son not mine who paid the price that day
How can I thank you for all that you have done?
Then I hear you whisper ... just love my son

And when I turned away from darkness, I heard the angel say it's done
And then the shadows fell behind me as I turned to face your son
For I can feel the passion and I can see what you have done
And I will love your people God and I will love your son

I was/am a huge AC/DC fan (Rock n Roll!) and I took the idea of this song from one of theirs and turned it on its head. Can you imagine travelling "Angel Class with Jesus by your side"? TWA ... Travelling With Angels!

I wish people would stop trying to be someone/something else and be who God made them to be. They would then reach their full potential, be totally unique and have talents, qualities and gifts that no one else has or will ever have. How awesome is that?

I also get really impatient (sorry!) with people who could physically do something to make a real difference in people's lives, but decide to offer the easy "I'll pray for you" option instead. I'm not suggesting that prayer is not important or powerful, it is, but sometimes we need to act and act quickly.

Yes, sometimes we need to comfort the disturbed. But sometimes we need to disturb the comfortable!

Well the Lord is my shepherd, that's all I need to know
When I go astray He leads me back His way
Where the peaceful waters flow
Every sinner has future like every saint has had a past
And it's no disgrace, yes it's my kind of race
Where the first will come in last

But on the highway to heaven it's going to be one hell of a ride
But at least I'll be travelling angel class
With Jesus by my side

He won't weed them and reap, but he will read them and weep
Because my story makes Him cry
You know the greatest failure in the world today
Is the failure not to try
I have told Him stories from the heart of the streets
And the street's inside my heart
Now He's heard everything He's forgiven my sin
And my journey is about to start

On the highway to heaven it's going to be one hell of a ride
But at least I'll be travelling angel class
With Jesus by my side

You know you can't go back because back's not there anymore
Unless I am mistaken
And stop trying to be like somebody else
That job's already taken
Please don't tell me that you'll pray for me
And that you need more time for thinking
Don't tell me that you'll take it on board
Because your boat's already sinking

But on the highway to heaven you can enjoy one hell of a ride
And at least you'll be travelling angel class
With Jesus by your side

The Albums

Cold and Roofless
Michael McMillan
https://itun.es/gb/W0-LG

Faith to Faith
Michael McMillan
https://itun.es/gb/vCHLG

Meet Me At The Cross
Michael McMillan
https://itun.es/gb/52hIR

Useful Links

www.alpha.org

www.glasgowelim.org.uk

www.greenviewevangelicalchurch.co.uk

www.glasgowcitymission.com

www.teenchallenge.org.uk

www.salt-and-light.org.uk

www.eatacd.com

www.essgeeproductions.co.uk